The Definition of Perseverance

A collection of poems

Nevone Blount

DEDICATION

Dedicated to my grandparents Odell and Shirley
Berry, Sean Washington and others that I've
loved who are not here carnally but still exist
spiritually.

Cages

I know why the caged bird sings
I know why the caged bird screams
I know why the caged bird cries
Tell me if the caged bird flies

This Morning

I left my terrors
on the nightstand

next to a ring
that I found
last week in an
empty parking lot.

I ran there
from past aspirations
that sprouted from
dead attempts

to sew my dreams
back together.

I found a heart
shaped locket
in a dumpster
behind the dorms

as I was searching
for my pride.

It reminded me
that even in the midst
of garbage

hope can
be found.

Letter To The Sky

I wrote a letter to the sky saying
thank you.
I placed it in a time capsule
and buried it in my backyard,
only to be dug up
when I made it to the top
of this mountain.

Struggle makes precious stones,
flawless and pure without
any residue from the dirt
that they were packed under.

Struggle makes the heart beat
stronger makes the heart beat longer.
The lungs have the ability to inhale
more perseverance and exhale failure.

So I wanted to tell the sky
thank you
for introducing me
to struggle.

It's been a match
made in heaven.

Circles

Run, young man, run.
To run to
something
is to run away
from another.

But what if
what you
were running from
you found yourself
running to?

Circles rotate around
and around
like spirals.
Your world becomes
a spiraling staircase.
Twisting and winding.
Twisted and winded.

Is it going
up or down?
Running
to and fro from
here to there
and back
again.

We're back

Again.

One day
we will stop
running.

Acceptance

The things we do
for acceptance
The things we do
for attention
The things we do
for affection
are all the same.

If mirrors could see
past our skin
then we would realize
that all of the

acceptance
attention
affection

that we need
is already there.

Don't Clip My Wings

Just give me my wings
so that I can fly
not into
but past the sky.

Let me dwell amongst stars
and other celestial bodies
and the moons

Don't let me come down
too soon.

Life is the ultimate drug
It can give me a high
or be a depressant;
weighing me down
or raising me past the sky.

Life, lift me higher
past the sky.

Want/Need

Here's a revelation:

The world can give
me nothing
that I need

only that
that I want.

If my needs come
from somewhere
otherworldly

then my needs
should become
what I want.

Life

Life is not
a fairy tale.
It never happens
the way we write it.

Life is not reality.

Reality is harsh.
Reality is cold.
Reality is painful.

Life is truth.
Life is joy.
Life is love.

Life is beauty even
though reality can be ugly.

Window Pain

I look out of my window pane
I see joy and pain
Sometimes I see the sun
Sometimes I see the rain

I look out of my window pane
I see the joy and the pain
Lord, can you take these
things off my brain?

Pieces of a Man

Pieces of a man
sprawled out on
the office floor

Tell the secretary
to schedule the meeting
for 10 AM

Pieces of a man
spread across
ghetto corridors

Tell the children
that daddy can't
make it home tonight

Pieces of a man
left on the courtyard
near the student union

Tell the instructor
that he'll be about
five minutes late today

Pieces of a man that fall
through the cracks of society
through the holes of a system
that doesn't want him
unless he is whole

yet won't help him
to achieve this goal.

Pieces of a man for all
of us to sweep up.

Liquid Dreams

Over time
you may come to realize
that dreams
are too often deferred.

Raisins in the sun
exist everywhere
not just Harlem

Raisins can't return
to the grapes
they once were

to make the wine
they were once meant
to make

Still Standing

The Lord is my light and salvation; whom shall I fear? The Lord is the strength of my life; of whom shall I be afraid?
Psalm 27:1

I was asked

How do you let go of your fears?
By unballing my fist full of tears.
By letting go of the pain that's developed over the years.

I've slipped and fell and heard my enemies cheer.
I've been beaten and left in the mud by so called peers.
Life has felt like a vehicle that I'm not equipped to steer.

Bleed out the pain that's developed through the years.
Release the doves from my fistful of tears.
These are the ways that I escape fear.

Cages 2

I know that the caged bird
waits
and waits
to be freed
or to escape

Tell me if the caged bird
flies.

I, Too

Inspired by Langston Hughes

I, too, sing America
but mine is an anthem
that you refuse to hear

for fear of understanding
something that you've
long avoided.

I, too, have songs, America,
songs of gospel, jazz and blues,
songs of inspiration and hope.

Songs inspired by ancestors
who beat on Djembe drums
before you beat on their backs,
America.

I, too, am America.
Just of a darker complexion
because of a darker past.

Hear my song.
Hear my voice.

I, too, sing America.

Am I America Enough?

Maybe I'm not permitted
to ignite fireworks
on the 4th of every July
although I liturgically stood
every day with my classmates
in grade school and began a chant
of "I pledge allegiance…"

although my past was spent
in your green fields picking
white cotton until red appeared
on my black fingertips

Yet still
treated as an outsider.
Maybe I'm not home

after all.

Greed

The world is black and white
and green.

Money talks.
Poverty walks

into museums
disguised as stores

because poverty can't afford
it can only marvel.

Poverty cleans hospitals
that it can never
get treatments in.

Poverty constructs homes
that it will never be able
to live in.

It is not racist.
It is not sexist.

Poverty is the neighbor
that you never step outside
to check on.

Body Language

You're good at reading body
language? What's that body
lying in the street saying?

Can you tell what that young
man with his pistol hanging
from his pants is saying?

What about that young lady
whose breast are trying to
escape her blouse?

Those tears rolling down
the children's faces
all speak different phrases

there's a tear for cold winter
nights and hot summer mornings;
there's a tear that asks if
daddy will ever make it home;
there's a tear that searches
high and low for hope.

You're good at reading body language.
What are those bodies saying?

Black History

Our history
His story
Her story
My story

But they try to turn my history
into some sort of fairy tale
like saying that we're all either
in or headed toward jail.

Our history
His story
Her story
My story

Tell the whole truth about
how much my people gave.
My history isn't limited
to civil rights and slaves.

Our history
His story
Her story
My story

Black women are more than just
a big butt and a smile.
Every Black man won't
have to face a criminal trial.

Our history
His story
Her story
My story

The Future

I see the blank stares on the kids'
faces. It's because their empty stomachs are
telling them more than their daddy ever
told them. The same one you pushed to
the side at five years old will rob you by twelve
and by sixteen will be doing drive bys. Feed them
this garbage about being an athlete or
an entertainer and wonder why his ball
and bail gets picked up more than his books.

Young girls wearing tight clothes and
yelling *If you like it then you should've
put a ring on it.* In fact, she's putting
a ring on a lifestyle of being with
various guys with or without a Lifestyle.
You smiled when they were younger
and bought them pants with messages
on the back and wonder why she opens
her legs more than she opens her brain.

Suit and Tie

Can someone please tell the suit
and tie that he can try
but he can't experience
project pain until he see
the world from the eyes
of those looking from behind
project window panes

The furthest some of them will
go will be out of their mind
Out of mind, out of sight
children of the night that fight
just to put a few bread crumbs
in their stomach - and you
couldn't stomach to walk
a mile in their hand-me-down shoes

You would rather get them handed
sentences - not the kind read
in books but the kinds that are
in the books thrown at them

Suit and tie, can you spare
a brother some change?
Can you give your brother
some change?
Suit and tie, do you even
have any change?

Do you know what change is?

I'm Black

I'm Black
but somewhere someone decide to call me
Negro, coon, jiggaboo, colored
Nigger, Nigga.

I'm Black
so they figured that my history, my
heritage, my ancestory was not important.
Or non existant.

I'm Black
so I was taught that I'm expected to be a
rapper, a pimp, a whore, an addict, an alchie.
Or if I'm lucky, an athlete.

I'm Black
so I was told that my sisters are only good
for sex, my brothers only good to slave.
I'm good for nothing.

I'm Black
so my future is already decided but I
didn't make the decision.
I'm headed for the grave or prison.

I'm Black
so education is optional but options are limited.
I'm a statistic waiting to happen and they will
try to make me happen.

But through the blood, the tears and the pain
I rise, I stand, I survive.
I'm unbreakable, unshakable, unmovable because
I'm Black.

The Deaths of Hip Hop

Spirits poured out on the concrete
by breathing zombies that still
inhabit despondent project buildings

Another news story of a 15 year old
shot on the 3rd story of his tenement
because hip hop's scriptures mandate
gunplay as the only way in his environment.

Ten crack commandments scribbled
on the staircase wall as another fiend
reaches out his hand to exchange his
heartbeat for a pebble from the sea
shore of death's ocean.

He dies slowly
the people die slower
crime rates increase
populations decrease

The alarm clock continues
yelling into deafened ears.
The snooze button has been pressed
too many times.

In a Dream

Freedom and equality
went hand in hand.

No bondage and hate.
This is what I saw
in my dream.

Dr. King and J. Edgar Hoover
were taking in a baseball game
together

Adolf Hitler make a toast
at a Jewish boy's bar mitzvah.

I saw it all
in a dream.

Negro Spiritual

In the back of my mind I hear
the old hymns sung by plantation
workers displaced from their families
hoping that their sweet chariot

will swing low enough to carry
them to heaven; carry them home.
I imagine that there was unshakeable
faith within those southern fields

surrounded by God's graces. Every
note taking them one step closer
to a freedom that couldn't be
found above the Mason Dixie Line;

a freedom that could only
be found above the clouds alongside
the angels in the presence
of the Almighty. Those

chosen children of Israel
believed that they would
cross the Red Sea without
as much as a sprinkle

of salt water on their feet.
The true definition of
perseverance. A trait far removed
from these modern day gentiles.

Neighborhood Watch

Dedicated to the memory of Trayvon Martin

When you read this poem
make sure that you read it
Black enough for your teacher

When you walk through
a gated community at night
make sure that you don't walk
too Black to be gunned down

When America wakes up (hopefully)
make sure that it knows
that racism isn't a distant
memory but an ugly reminder
of work that remains undone

Work that remains ignored, murders
of blacks being treated like dirt
swept under a rug. Not realizing that
after too much dirt, the rug will begin
to rise, exposing what's under

I knew that the rifle
was still pointed at the
balcony of the Lorraine
Motel, shooting down
our Kings

Now I see that they are still
throwing our princes in the
Tallahatchie River

I see that we are black
enough to be illiterate
welfare babies only capable
of committing crimes

But we are too black
to be intelligent or successful
and worth anything more
than just three-fifths of a population.

Make sure that your teacher knows
that you are black enough to read
this poem and that blackness runs
deeper than just skin color.

Beach Chair

Life's a beach
so I spend most
of my days building

sand castles for paper
queens who are only
concerned with the amount

of paper in my jeans
or where I work
or what I drive

Impressing them is impossible
It would be easier to count
the grains of sand
that I'm walking on

Darker Berries

Maybe if my skin tone
was a few shades
lighter

then you and I would
be skipping class right now
to take in a matinee
and then brunch at IHOP.

But your eyes couldn't match
your emotions and you couldn't
see yourself with someone so
BLACK

Fortunately for me
I couldn't see myself
with someone so ugly.

Untouchable

Fine art in a gallery
is not to be touched.
Not for fear of fingerprints
but because its viewers
can't fully comprehend
what they are beholding.

You are like a mannequin.
Breathtaking in all
of your features with captivating
beauty able to stop any man
in the midst of his stride to say
"Wow"
Yet something that only
my eyes can experience while
my mind wonders if
plastic dreams come true too.

You take me back
to my childhood
when I looked at the stars
light years away.
I reach out for you
but pull back only air.

Air
the air
his air.
Some day, some man
will need

you
only you
right there.

While I'll still be looking
reaching out past the
"Do Not Touch" sign.

Emotionless

She feels as if her life
stops when the music stops.
The only life that she knows
is being the life of the party.

Empty red cups replace
empty spaces where her
heart once lied; ripped
out by countless lies told.

She reaches to the depths
of long-neck bottles hoping
that Jose Cuervo and Jack
Daniels can tell her something
to ease her pains.

But they are silent.

Nowhere

You appeared out of nowhere
like a figment of my imagination
or something that I only saw
when I slumbered.

Just as quickly
you decided
that you were fed up
with my world

and returned
to nowhere.

She Killed Chivalry

She murdered chivalry.
Bang. Bang.
Two shots to chivalry's chest.

In the midst of resuscitation
Bang.
One more shot to chivalry's head.

I tried to resurrect him
but she wouldn't allow it.

Back to Reality

Dancing with you on sandy
stages, the waves serving
as the soundtrack. The moon
as our spotlight, entertaining
the stars as our audience.

Every word that escapes
your mouth embeds
itself into my ears;
as beautiful as those
written by Neruda.

And you, my dream, are
as pure as heavenly
choirs strumming my soul's
chords like the angels' fingers
gliding across harp strings.

But you, my dream, are
just a cerebral glimpse.
Trapped in my mind
with the inability to be
released. An episode forever
syndicated in my own imagination.

Shooting Stars

I used to wish
upon the shooting
stars in your eyes

until I realized
that wishes
in a wishing
well didn't end well

You used to light
up dark backdrops
like stars in the sky

Then one day
all of the stars

fell.

Sun Shades

The girl at the stoplight
in the convertible with
the shades on

I wonder if
I wonder if
I wonder

if I can see past
her shades.

If she would let me into
the world that's hiding
behind the tint.

Are her shades
the only thing tinted?
Maybe her eyes
aren't the only things
she's trying to protect.

Once

You were once a beautiful
soul; a spirit so sweet
to be enjoyed by
not one but all
of those who came into
contact with your essence.

Once seems like so long ago.
Once was before the world
infiltrated your heart and turned
you into something that it wanted
you to be. Once was upon

us a time ago. If time
machines existed in poems
then this one would take
us back to that place called
Once. Then we could be
one like we once were.

Cold As Ice

Your love
is cold.

An icy sheet
lies over
your heart.

Your heart
is a glacier

sinking everything
that it comes into
contact with.

But revenge
is best served
cold
right?

So it all makes sense.

Close Enough

I remember you saying that you just wanted someone
who would dedicate their time and themselves to you
because that's what you would do for him. At that
moment I wanted to be the one to sign the deal that would
trade your discontent for moments of bliss.

We would slow jam and slow jam until the moon retired
from its shift and the sun took over watching the earth. I
realized that even if I had 27 hours in a day, it still
wouldn't be enough time.

You came close to touch but drew back quickly like a
child that touches a heated oven door; and like a child
awaiting the perfect present on Christmas morning, I
waited for you to arrive.

But you never did.

The News

My friends said you
were bad news.

I told them
that even bad
news needed
attention.

I paid so much attention
to you that I couldn't see
that you no longer wanted
to do this.

You're still breaking down
all of the guys deeming
you important enough
to invest time into

But no more
for me
no news
is good news

The Best Thing

You are
the best thing
that never happened
to me.

You've finally been released
from the prison of my mind.
I hope you
are happy now

because I am.

I don't think you wanted to tell.
I would've been your best kept secret.
Now I'm your most beautiful nightmare.

Sweet dreams, angel.

(S)End Button

Funny how fingers "accidentally" press send
buttons days after lips end relationships.

This is the type of party that you wish to throw?
A surprise party?

Don't surprise me too much because weak hearts
can't take too many sudden actions. Sudden death.

The next point wins but they don't tell you
that the next point ends.

The next point is the point of no return;
the point of no air. Is there any air up there,

Ms. High and Mighty? As you taste the sun
and allow the condensation from the clouds

to roll off your back. Allow the condensation
to roll the same way that those words

rolled off my tongue onto the dry, cracked bass
of your eardrums. What tune were you hearing?

You were so used to hearing about how beautiful
you were that my words were being thrown into
a discard pile next to phrases such as
"So do you have a man?"

But I wasn't about that.
I was about...
I was about to...

I was about to let you know before
you accidentally pressed end.

Writer's Block

The blank page
troubles my soul
and haunts me
turning me into
an insomniac

It's frightening
white space
no words
It's horror

more maddening than
an Edgar Allan Poe story
more terrifying than
a Stephen King novel

I wonder if God felt this
before writing the universe

When The Clouds Cry

When the clouds cry, I hear the angels' voices.
Their melodies gently soothe my soul.
They tell me that I'm protected.
I know that better days are ahead.

My soul is soothed by their gentle melodies.
Voices from heaven reassuring my confidence.
I can see better days in my future.
The abundance of life is in clear view.

Reassurance of my confidence from heavenly voices
that leave footprints upon my heart.
I can clearly see life's abundance.
It will all be worth it in the end.

The footprints that have been left on my heart.
The glow that's been left within my spirit.
The end is worthy of the struggle.
I heard the angel's voices through the clouds' cries.

Heaven At Night

A place where the demons
knock but I don't deal
with that. My angels run
to the door for me instead.

A place where fear
is nonexistent. All intimidation,
trepidation is gone.
Failure is dead.

A place that doesn't know
darkness. Even the gray clouds
are beautiful. My soul
is tranquil and everything is right.

A place that my spirit runs
for refuge; my mind's
emporium. I play with
my dreams in Heaven at night.

Should I Admit

Should I admit
that I still get
teary eyed when I see
a father with his son?
Cause we didn't really
get a chance to do that
sort of thing.

      Why

would a man leave
a woman with three sons

would a man walk
into darkness and dissolve
into a memory or a fantasy

would a man make
a selfish decision

One in which he reveled
in its rewards but disregarded
its consequences.

They
Them
He
Him

I imagined
this is what
we became
to you.

But I became a man
that had to do away
with childish things
childish thoughts
childhood nightmares.

Should I admit
that it was difficult
to forgive

but I did.

Girl Friend

She began selling her body
claiming it's her body
and she ain't hurting
no body

She said she was just tired
of feeling like a
nobody

I used to love her
I still do
just parts of her now

In high school, after class
I would go to her house
and laugh at old reruns of
"A Different World"

Now we live in different worlds
Hers seeming to have no association
with feelings or emotions

I can't help but to still love her
because that's what friends are for
To be first hand witnesses
to your self destruction

Still loving you the same

Voicemail

In a 2 minute voicemail
all I heard was *I need
to talk to you.* If I

would've seen the signs
earlier, then maybe I would
be a better man today.

Today I finally realized
that you were seeking
help to be a better man;

In that quest to find help
I see that I need you just
as much as you need me.

I see that you are
helping me
find myself

Moments

The moments that create hours
The hours that create days
The days that create life

Moments that were given that
we wish we could have back.

Some moments that we wish to forget
but somehow always seem to remember.

Moments that are meant to destroy us
actually build us up as high as the clouds.

Moments to weep. Moments to smile.
Moments of pain. Moments of joy.

Moments to be spent as if they were our last
because the very next moment could be that.

Ambition

She was more concerned
with what guys
were driving
rather

than what was driving them.

To no fault of her own –
you can't tell the bank
teller that you wish
to withdraw
some ambition
to pay your mortgage.

Ambition with a side
of perseverance
washed down
with a cup of aspiration

isn't enough to quiet
the rumbling stomach.

Ambition is, however,
a parasite
that leeches onto a few

and forces its host
to continue to drive
even if they are driving

nothing.

Memories (Faded)

Looking toward the future
holding on to the past.

Dark nights leading us
into overcast mornings.

Mourning the times
that used to bring joy.

The things that we used to be laughed
over are now bringing tears.

Do you remember the memories?
Are you just forgetting present?

Are you chasing something
or running from something?

Life   is   a   vapor.
Don't get caught in the mist.

Black Keys

The black keys on the piano
have the most to say

Let them speak to me
say all that you can to me
through them

Say all that you can
while I'm still here
to hear

Because one day
unbeknownst to us

we will leave this place
and be laid to rest under
the sound of the tinkling

black keys.

Continue On

I've risen from a nightmare
only to discover that all along
it has been a dream. A story
to be told to the masses about
trial and error and tribulation
and redemption, retribution, imprisonment,
execution. The old man must die time
and time again. The old way must cease
so that we can live in peace. It's
difficult to be at peace when you
only have a piece of mind. The rest
you can't find but God finds it somewhere
in the bowels of the earth and He picks
it up and polishes it to something new
and original and the people that thought
they knew you just sit and marvel
at the new you. They won't admit
it but some of them threw you to
the dogs a long time ago because
to them, you couldn't show, you couldn't
prove what was going on within you.
The old ladies in church would sing
Something's got a hold of meeee
But what is that something? It's in
that last piece of mind that makes you
lose sleep over some things. Those somethings
are little things that grow to big things
and cause you to not be able to see anything.
Anything. Everything. Something.
Are all the same thing in the end.

This too shall pass but that's quicksand
in the hourglass dropping grains one by
one with each grain landing sound like
a hit on a bass drum. I was just thinking
and sinking further and farther.
The light in the tunnel just got darker
and darker. At night, hoping
that the tears in my eyes could provide
the gasoline necessary to take flight.
Cause these ol' eyes and this ol' heart
has lost sight of what it was on
from the start. All along in the mind
you hear. Press. Press. Press.
Toward the mark of the high
calling but how can this be done when
I'm bawling and I see them balling.
They're on the court and I'm in
the stands; both of us making it rain
but my rain is hitting my hands from
my eyes. Dry up this river
that's flowing up from my heart
and into my brain and through
my ducts and onto this page
and onto the stage. Of life.
Life is a game that can't be won
until the buzzer goes off.
We just have to adjust to every quarter.

Cages - The Finale

Will the caged bird
ever reach its
full potential?

Tell the caged bird
that if it's not released

to free itself and fly
fly
fly

toward its freedom.